MY FRIENDS EAT PORK

····· WHAT ABOUT ME? ·····

All rights reserved.

No part of this book may be reproduced, transmitted, or stored in an information retrieval system in any form or by any means, graphic, electronic, or mechanical, including photocopying, taping, and recording, without prior written permission from the author.

Copyright © 2019 Bachar Karroum

ISBN: 978-1-988779-11-9

Dépôt légal : bibliothèque et archives nationales du Québec, 2019.
Dépôt légal : bibliothèque et archives Canada, 2019.

Author : **Bachar Karroum**
Illustrator : **Tanja Varcelija**
Graphic Designer : **Samuel Gabriel**
Cover Designer : **Rebeca Covers**
Proofreader : **Christina Cutting**

In the name of God!

This is little Ahmad. He is six.

Ahmad is a Muslim boy who loves being surrounded by his friends and family.

Ahmad lives with his mother, father, and his sister Amina.

His best friends are Jack, Liz, and George.

Today is a special day. It's Jack's birthday and Ahmad is going to his party.

On the table, there is a wide spread of food of different shapes and colors.

Ahmad notices some ham and cheese sandwiches. Ahmad knows he should not eat ham. So, he skips the sandwich.

"But why are my friends eating ham sandwiches?" he wonders.

The next day, Ahmad attends the annual event at school with his sister Amina.

There are many stands with a variety of foods for sale. At the burger stand, Ahmad chooses a delicious-looking burger.

Amina notices some bacon on it, so she asks for two burgers without bacon.

"But why are other kids eating bacon?" Ahmad says to himself.

The next weekend, Ahmad and his parents go out to a restaurant.

When it's time to order, Ahmad wants the same tasty-looking pizza as he sees on the next table. However, he notices some pepperoni on it.

Ahmad knows he can't eat pepperoni. So, he asks for a vegetarian pizza.

"But, why is this family allowed to eat pepperoni?" Ahmad is a little annoyed.

Back at school on Monday, during lunch, Ahmad sees his friend George eating a ham sandwich, while Liz is enjoying a slice of pepperoni pizza and Jack is having a burger with bacon.

Ahmad is in dismay. "My friends eat ham, pepperoni, and bacon!

I know I am Muslim, but why can't I ?!" thinks Ahmad, very confused.

While visiting his grandparents, Ahmad seeks his grandma's help.

"What is it my boy?" Grandma asks.

"Grandma, why don't we eat bacon, pepperoni or ham in our family?"

"Good question, Ahmad. I'm glad you asked. It's because…

…as you know, we are Muslims.

Being Muslim is about submitting ourselves to Allah, meaning that we should follow His guidance.

In the holy Quran, Allah says it is forbidden to eat pork.

Pork is the meat of the pig. Bacon, pepperoni, and ham are pork meat."

"But why doesn't Allah want us to eat pork meat?" asks Ahmad.

"You know, Ahmad, it is mentioned four times in the Quran that we cannot eat pork. We therefore understand the importance of this prohibition.

However, Allah doesn't provide an explanation. Allah knows what is good and what is not good for us. We must trust Him and believe His words...that is what we call faith."

"But Grandma, why do my friends eat pork then?" Ahmad enquires.

"You are a Muslim, Ahmad, but some of your friends are not.

And their religion may not forbid them from eating pork," Grandma replies.

"But Grandma … don't we all have the same God?

Why is it OK for my friends?" Ahmad asks.

"That is an excellent question, Ahmad.

There is surely a good reason why it's allowed in some religions.

Only God really knows the answer to your question.

Allah, the Almighty, knows what we do not know.

"You must also know that Allah and His messenger, Prophet Muhammad (peace be upon him), tell us to respect other religions.

So even if your friends eat pork, you must not judge, criticize, or hold any grudges against them."

Ahmad is comforted. He now understands that having faith means believing in the words of God.

He knows why, as a Muslim, he should not eat pork meat.

He also knows not to criticize others if they do so.

Ahmad feels it in his heart that following God's guidance is the right thing to do.

I hope you and your children enjoyed the story!

Stay tuned for the next books.

Printed in Poland
by Amazon Fulfillment
Poland Sp. z o.o., Wrocław